Renew
Your Mind

21-Day Mind Renewal
Volume 1: Romans 12

Tools and resources to help you
SIMPLY go DEEP in your relationship with God.

www.ButGodMinistry.com

 @butGodMinistry
@Jesus365.devo

 @_butGod
@Jesus365.devo

...but God

Available in App Stores

Contents

21-Day Mind Renewal

Do not be **conformed**
to this **world,**
but be **transformed**
by the **renewal**
of your **mind,**
that by **testing**
you may **discern**
what is the **will of God,**
what is **good**
and **acceptable**
and **perfect.**

Romans 12:2

Renew Your Mind

21-Day Mind Renewal

You are created by the hands of God, with the breath of God, in the image and likeness of God (Genesis 1:27). The human mind is like no other created thing. In the beautiful creation that is your mind, God has given you the ability to think, study, analyze, process, ponder, store into memory, reframe, and so much more. There is unfathomable potential available to you.

When God's word says to renew your mind (Romans 12:2), it is because God knows you have the ability to do this. He created this ability in you. But it takes focus, commitment, and intentionality. Without these things, you will simply drift with the current of the culture and the loud voices all around you. Without intention, you will simply conform to the patterns of the world. The result? You will live a life outside of God's perfect design and will for you, you will believe the lies of the enemy over the truth of God, you will experience anxiety and unrest from striving and spinning your wheels on the things of the world. But a renewed mind transforms. A renewed mind discerns the perfect will of God, believes who God says you are, walks in sync with God and the plans He created in advance for you, experiences oneness with God, joy, contentment, peace. Sounds amazing, right?

You have the ability to control what you choose to think about. What you let in your mind. How you process what goes into your mind. What your reaction will be. There are countless studies and incredible science demonstrating that God's desire for you to renew your mind isn't just some lofty, unrealistic idea, but instead a reality built into the magnificent intricacies of your brain and how it functions. These things God tells us about renewing our mind, experiencing peace, finding contentment in all things...these things are possible and part of how God created you. If you are interested in a deeper dive into a study of the brain, I recommend checking out *Switch on Your Brain* by Dr. Caroline Leaf, a Christian neuroscientist. Many of the concepts included in this 21-day study are based on her mind-renewal research with incredibly impressive results.

In this 21-day study, you will dive deep into Romans 12 while also practicing habits to begin a journey toward renewing your mind. Friend, it is only 21 days. You can do it. Stick with it and trust the process. If you want change, you have to be willing to change. Commit to 20-30 minutes a day of focused mind renewal and watch transformation unfold, as God promises it will.

Why Romans 12? First and foremost, the biggest part of renewing your mind is setting it on God's Word. As such, your 21-day mind-renewal process should include time in Scriptures. Romans 12 contains the verse that tells us, "Do not be conformed to this world, but be transformed by the renewal of your mind, that by testing you may discern what is the will of God, what is good and acceptable and perfect." (Romans 12:2).

The book of Romans is a beautiful presentation of the Gospel by Paul. Romans chapters 1-8 include the foundation of Christian faith and why all of us, as sinful people, need a savior. On your own, you can't save yourself. The good news is Jesus is that perfect Savior and there is so much freedom for you who believe. There is no condemnation for you in Christ Jesus. You. Are. Free.

Romans chapters 9-11 explains God's sovereignty over all and how if you confess with your mouth that Jesus is Lord and believe in your heart that God raised him from the dead, you will be saved (Romans 10:9-10)... you can say, "yes, I believe that Jesus is Lord, He died for me and God raised Him from the dead." And in doing so, you can experience that forgiveness of sins, salvation, restoration, and freedom.

Romans chapter 12 – the focus of this 21-day devotional journal – follows with how you should then live as one who has been saved by Jesus. Your life, your priorities, your MINDSET should be different, given this extravagant love and freedom you have been given.

Through this study, we pray you will fill your mind with truth, replacing any thoughts that are hindering living your best life...the life God designed for you to walk in for such a time as this. You are here on purpose for a purpose. You are exactly where you are in this season for a reason. Allow God to fill your mind with His truth, guidance, and direction. Seek to journey along the perfect path He has created for you.

● ● ●

21-Day Assignment

For 21-days we invite you to set aside focused time each day – about 20-30 minutes – to complete the following seven steps based on Scriptural references. This is not intended to be a magical formula, but rather a time of intention to recognize and capture thoughts not of God that are keeping you from living your best life that God has created for you for such a time as this.

Set your alarm early, grab a cup of coffee or tea and devote your first minutes of the day to renewing your mind. Space is provided each day to walk through the seven steps.

The following pages include a description of what you will be doing each day, along with Scriptural support for each.

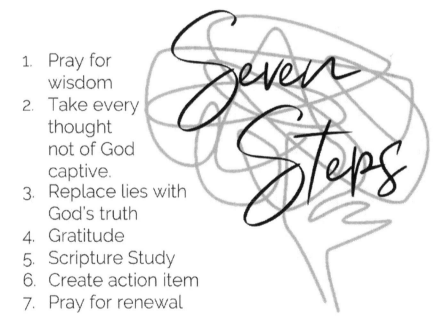

1. Pray for wisdom
2. Take every thought not of God captive.
3. Replace lies with God's truth
4. Gratitude
5. Scripture Study
6. Create action item
7. Pray for renewal

Seek God first. Abide in Him. Begin with a short prayer. Ask God to give you wisdom and understanding. Ask Him to change your desires to match His and to join you in renewing your mind to be transformed more and more into the image of Jesus. If you don't know where to begin, we have included a prayer you can recite in the next section (p. 15) to help you get started. Your prayers don't have to be complicated works of poetic art, but rather a heartfelt conversation with God.

"For I know the plans I have for you, declares the LORD, plans for welfare and not for evil, to give you a future and a hope. **Then you will call upon me and come and pray to me, and I will hear you.** You will seek me and find me, when you seek me with all your heart." Jeremiah 29:11-13

"**If any of you lacks wisdom, let him ask God, who gives generously to all without reproach, and it will be given him.** But let him ask in faith, with no doubting, for the one who doubts is like a wave of the sea that is driven and tossed by the wind." James 1:5-6

"In my distress I called upon the LORD; to my God I cried for help. From his temple **he heard my voice, and my cry to him reached his ears.**" Psalm 18:6

"And Jesus answered them, '**Have faith in God**.Truly, I say to you, whoever says to this mountain, 'Be taken up and thrown into the sea,' and does not doubt in his heart, but **believes that what he says will come to pass**, it will be done for him. Therefore I tell you, whatever you ask in prayer, **believe that you have received it**, and it will be yours.'" Mark 11:22-24

Take Every Thought Not of God Captive (5 minutes)

This is an important step not to be taken lightly or brushed over. Capture any toxic, anxious or negative thoughts. Search your heart for any sinful patterns or desires. Dig deep to examine any idols taking up a higher position in your life than God. Rather than suppress or ignore these things, bring them to the surface so you can replace them with God's truth and God's will.

What voices are you listening to that are dragging you down and leaving you paralyzed? Here's a good rule of thumb to think through the root of the words filling your mind:

God's voice will line up with Scripture. It stills, leads, restores, enlightens, encourages, comforts, uplifts, calms, and convicts. On the other hand,

Satan's voice rushes, pushes, frightens, confuses, discourages, worries, compares, obsesses, and condemns.

Reflect on the voices you hear in your mind. Are they in alignment with God's truth or the lies of the enemy? Take every thought not of God captive. Don't assume they will disappear on their own. There is a spiritual battle raging all around you and you must be intentional. Call the toxic thoughts out for the lie that they are or the impossible barrier they seem to be in your mind.

Sometimes the thoughts in our mind are rooted in sinful patterns and idols in our life we are clinging too more tightly than God. Are we fighting for control, for approval, for affirmation from others, for self-medication, for self-glorification, for respect at all costs? Are we elevating our social status, our family, our finances, our appearance, our career aspirations, our possessions above our relationship with and obedience to God?

Sin patterns and idols in our life often become so ingrained in our daily life and thought patterns that they become hard to recognize. Spend time in prayer asking God to reveal them to you. A quote I often reflect on is, "the level of your irritation often reveals the depth of your idolatry." In other words, pay attention to what gets you the most angry. Dig deep to understand the root of the anger. Is it rooted in an idol or sin pattern you are clinging too that is getting ruffled by another person or circumstance?

As you work through these 21-days of prayer, study, and reflection, you may find that you are working on one thought pattern the entire time. That is okay! It takes time and intention to change our thoughts and actions. That is what this intentional time is for.

"For though we walk in the flesh, we are not waging war according to the flesh. For the weapons of our warfare are not of the flesh but have **divine power to destroy strongholds**. We destroy arguments and every lofty opinion raised against the knowledge of God, and **take every thought captive to obey Christ**, being ready to punish every disobedience, when your obedience is complete." 2 Corinthians 10:3-6

"Anyone who does not love does not know God, because God is love….Love is patient and kind; **love does not** envy or boast; **it is not** arrogant or rude. **It does not** insist on its own way; **it is not** irritable or resentful; **it does not** rejoice at wrongdoing, but rejoices with the truth. Love bears all things, believes all things, hopes all things, endures all things." 1 John 4:8, 1 Corinthians 13:4-7

"**Be sober-minded; be watchful.** Your adversary the devil prowls around like a roaring lion, seeking someone to devour." 1 Peter 5:8

"He [Satan] was a murderer from the beginning, and does not stand in the truth, because there is no truth in him. When he lies, he speaks out of his own character, for **he is a liar and the father of lies**." John 8:44

"Do not love the world or the things in the world. If anyone loves the world, the love of the Father is not in him. **For all that is in the world— the desires of the flesh and the desires of the eyes and pride of life—is not from the Father but is from the world.** And the world is passing away along with its desires, but whoever does the will of God abides forever." 1 John 2:15-17

"The **thief comes only to steal and kill and destroy**. I came that they may have life and have it abundantly." John 10:10

"**Get behind me, Satan!** You are a hindrance to me. For you are not setting your mind on the things of God, but on the things of man." Matthew 16:33

Replace lies with truth (5 minutes)

Here is the freeing part, friends. We can replace the lies of the enemy and desires of the world with God's truth and God's plans. Remind yourself of God's truth. Remind yourself who God says you are. Remind yourself that God is with you. Remind yourself that God will fight for you. Remind yourself that God will provide for you. Remind yourself that following the things of God far surpass following the things of the world. Remind yourself how much God loves you. Remind yourself that God can do the impossible...in fact, He loves to do the impossible! Remind yourself that God is working even in the suffering, the hard, and the waiting. Let truth flood over every negative, anxious and toxic thought. Let God change your desires. Retrain your mind to focus instead on God's truth. You are so very loved by Him and He has such beautiful plans for you.

"But he said, '**What is impossible with man is possible with God**.'" Luke 18:27

"For **God hath not given us the spirit of fear**; but of power, and of love, and of a sound mind." 2 Timothy 1:7 (KJV)

"I can do **all things through Christ** who strengthens me." Philippians 4:13

"Do not be anxious about anything, but in everything by prayer and supplication with thanksgiving let your requests be made known to God. And **the peace of God, which surpasses all understanding, will guard your hearts and your minds in Christ Jesus**." Philippians 4:6-7

"Finally, brothers, whatever is **true**, whatever is **honorable**, whatever is **just**, whatever is **pure**, whatever is **lovely**, whatever is **commendable**, if there is any **excellence**, if there is anything **worthy of praise, think about these things**." Philippians 4:8

"But the fruit of the Spirit is **love, joy, peace, patience, kindness, goodness, faithfulness, gentleness, self-control**; against such things there is no law." Galatians 5:22-23

"Finally, be strong in the Lord and in the strength of his might. Put on the **whole armor of God**, that you may be able **to stand against the schemes of the devil**. For we do not wrestle against flesh and blood, but against the rulers, against the authorities, against the cosmic powers over this present darkness, against the spiritual forces of evil in the heavenly places." Ephesians 6:10-12

If you are struggling to replace the enemy's lies with God's truth, we have some verses listed by category to help you get started. Visit www.butGodMinistry.com/GodsTruth

4

Gratitude (1-2 minutes)

Part of renewing your mind and replacing lies of the world with truths of God is to focus on gratitude. Gratitude is a game-changer and perspective-shifter. God tells us to be grateful in all circumstances. Countless studies have been conducted showing the health and well-being benefits of documenting gratitude. Again, science and research are catching up to what God teaches us to do. Each day you will write 5 things you are grateful for.

"**Rejoice always**, pray without ceasing, **give thanks in all circumstances**; for this is the will of God in Christ Jesus for you." 1 Thessalonians 5:16-19

Study God's Word (5-10 minutes)

Filling your mind with God's truth – God's Word – and an abiding relationship with Him is foundational to renewing your mind. On this 21-day journey, you will be slowly going through Romans 12. Each passage is presented in the English Standard Version (ESV) translation as well as the Message (MSG) translation. Read it through a couple of times. Underline, highlight, doodle, and take notes as you read. Note transition words (so, therefore, by, but, instead, etc.). Jot down things you don't understand and want to look up later.

As you read the selected passage each day, slowly focus on God's truth and instruction. Let it soak in. Restate it. Wrestle with it. Ask yourself hard questions about it. Talk to God about it and ask Him to reveal Himself to you through His word. Questions to prompt your thinking accompany each day's passage. If you want to go a bit deeper or have questions about a passage, a great commentary to start with is David Guzik's Enduring Word which can be found at www.enduringword.com/bible-commentary/romans-12/

"But seek first the kingdom of God and his righteousness, and all these things will be added to you." Matthew 6:33

"Abide in me, and I in you. As the branch cannot bear fruit by itself, unless it abides in the vine, neither can you, unless you abide in me." John 15:4

Action Item (2-3 minutes)

Next you will write out one thing you are going to do that day to change your thought patterns, or focus on God first/more, or take a step in obedience you feel Him calling you to take, or to turn away from something He is telling you to turn from. It can be a small baby step...action in the right direction is progress. But I challenge you to really stretch yourself to the point where you know you need God to help you.

And it is okay if it is the same thing each of the 21 days. It takes time to change our thought patterns and resulting actions. The key is to do something. While reflective time with God is critically important, taking action is important too!

If you are struggling with your feelings not matching up with the truths you have inserted in place of the lies the enemy is filling your mind with, don't be discouraged. It takes time to uproot firmly planted lies. But you can do it and you will get there. Pray about even small steps you can take each day. Lean into the power of God to be able to do these things, and you can do these things before you feel these things. You can act like the person you want to become. It isn't faking, it is trusting God to come in and transform you.

"But **be doers of the word, and not hearers only, deceiving yourselves**." James 1:22

"Now that you know these things, **you will be blessed if you** do **them**." John 13:17

"**Whatever you do, work heartily, as for the Lord and not for men**, knowing that from the Lord you will receive the inheritance as your reward. You are serving the Lord Christ." Colossians 3:23-24
"I therefore, a prisoner for the Lord, urge you to **walk in a manner worthy of the calling to which you have been called**..." Ephesians 4:1

Closing Prayer (1-2 minutes)

Ask God to be with you in your action steps. Ask Him to expand your faith and belief that He can do the impossible. Thank God for His faithfulness. Thank Him in advance for the miracle of transformation He can't wait to do in your life through time with Him and the renewing of your mind.

"Now **to him who is able to do far more abundantly** than all that we ask or think, according to the **power at work within us**, to him be glory in the church and in Christ Jesus throughout all generations, forever and ever. Amen." Ephesians 3:20-21

Prayer

God, as I begin to spend time with you, I first thank you that you are above all things. That you are all-knowing, all-powerful, and always present. That you are a good good Father who wants good things for your children, including me. I thank you that I am your child; a beloved heir to your kingdom. I thank you that you have prepared good works in advance for me to walk in. I thank you for never leaving me and for fighting for me. I thank you that you are full of love, mercy, grace, and compassion. I thank you for the many gifts you have given me. Help me to use them well.

God, I ask you to give me wisdom where I am lacking. I ask you to fill those holes within me that were made for only you to fill. Empty me of the things I try to fill them with that are keeping me from the life you have created for me. Bring to mind anything that is not of you that is getting in the way...any negative thoughts, envy, strife, unforgiveness, insecurity, pride, anger, doubt, fear, anxiety...any of it, God. And guide me in replacing these things with your truth. Point me to your truth. God, help me to renew my mind and to be transformed more and more into the perfect image of your precious Son, Jesus. God, change my "want to". Give me a deep desire to want to know you more; to want to spend time with you; to want to believe your truth over the lies of the world. Open my heart, mind, and soul to hear you... and give me the faith and courage to be obedient.

God, I am expectant and I thank you in advance for the miracle you will do in my mind and my life.

In the mighty name of Jesus. Amen.

Search me, O God,
and know **my heart**!
Try me and know
my thoughts!
And see if there be
any grievous way in me,
and **lead me** in
the way everlasting!

Psalm 139: 23-24

Renew Your Mind

21-Days of Mind Renewal
Volume 1: Romans 12 Study

Before you begin, make sure you read over the previous section (p. 7-14) describing the seven steps to complete each day.

Day 1: _____

1 Pray for wisdom & mind renewal.

You can use the prayer on page 15 as a starting point if you aren't sure where to begin.

2 Take every thought not of God Captive.

What toxic thoughts, worries, anxieties, fears, sin struggles, impossible barriers are standing in your way today? What is currently taking first place in your life over God? Jot your notes down below and put them in the left hand columns on the following page.

_____

_____

_____

_____

_____

3 Replace the lies with God's truth and Word.

In the right hand column on the following page, insert God's truth in place of lies or worldly patterns you captured. Space is also provided to journal below as you capture these thoughts/patterns and give them to God. Take time to Google "Bible verses about _____" (fear, anxiety, depression, pain, loss, insecurity, pride, unforgiveness, etc.) if you need to look up a truth about something you are struggling with. We also have some verses by category at www.butGodMinistry.com/GodsTruth

_____

_____

_____

_____

_____

_____

Thoughts/patterns not of God	God's TRUTH to claim/overcome

Reflect upon the following in your life right now:
(Jot down any that apply that you can think of in these categories from Philippians 4:8)

What is...	
True Honorable Just Pure Lovely Commendable Excellent Praiseworthy	

4 Five things I am grateful for today:

1. _____

2. _____

3. _____

4. _____

5. _____

5 Today's Scripture – Romans 12:1

I appeal to you therefore, brothers, by the mercies of God, to present your bodies as a living sacrifice, holy and acceptable to God, which is your spiritual worship. (ESV)

So here's what I want you to do, God helping you: Take your everyday, ordinary life—your sleeping, eating, going-to-work, and walking-around life—and place it before God as an offering. Embracing what God does for you is the best thing you can do for him. (MSG)

Underline, highlight, doodle your initial thoughts and notes as you read the passage.

Paul's "therefore" or "so" refers back to the chapters preceding this one (Romans 1-11). In these chapters, Paul lays out the sin in all of us, our desperate need for a savior, the sovereignty of God, the salvation found through Jesus by confessing and believing that He is Lord...that He died on the cross and it counted for us...that He was raised from the dead...that He took on our sins and gave us His righteousness. We can't save ourselves, in fact, what we don't want to do we do and what we want to do we don't do. We are hopeless when left to ourselves to save us. BUT GOD. God made a way through Jesus. There is therefore now no condemnation for those of us who believe in Him. In God's sovereignty and perfect timing, He made a way for you to be made right with Him. As a believer saved by the blood of Jesus, when God see you, He sees Jesus. This is the foundational truth from which Paul transitions into Romans 12:1.

What is Paul's "therefore" (ESV) or "so" (MSG) expected response for you as a believer in today's Romans 12:1 passage?

_____

_____

_____

How do we do this?

By the _____ of God. (ESV)
God _____ you. (MSG)

What does "mercy" mean (it's okay if you have to look it up)?

_____

_____

_____

What are the mercies of God? What do they look like? How will they help us?

_____

_____

_____

_____

_____

How then should we live according to Paul in Romans 12:1? What does this practically look life in our lives?

_____

_____

_____

_____

_____

6 Take action.

What is one thing you can do today to go take action with regard to your new way of thinking (from steps 2 and 3)?

_____

_____

_____

_____

_____

_____

_____

7 Close in prayer, thanking God in advance for renewal and transformation.

● ● ●

Day 2: _____

1 Pray for wisdom & mind renewal.

You can use the prayer on page 15 as a starting point if you aren't sure where to begin.

2 Take every thought not of God Captive.

What toxic thoughts, worries, anxieties, fears, sin struggles, impossible barriers are standing in your way today? What is currently taking first place in your life over God? Jot your notes down below and put them in the left hand columns on the following page.

_____

_____

_____

_____

_____

3 Replace the lies with God's truth and Word.

In the right hand column on the following page, insert God's truth in place of lies or worldly patterns you captured. Space is also provided to journal below as you capture these thoughts/patterns and give them to God. Take time to Google "Bible verses about _____" (fear, anxiety, depression, pain, loss, insecurity, pride, unforgiveness, etc.) if you need to look up a truth about something you are struggling with. We also have some verses by category at www.butGodMinistry.com/GodsTruth

_____

_____

_____

_____

_____

Thoughts/patterns not of God God's TRUTH to claim/overcome

Reflect upon the following in your life right now:

(Jot down any that apply that you can think of in these categories from Philippians 4:8)

What is...	
True Honorable Just Pure Lovely Commendable Excellent Praiseworthy	

4 Five things I am grateful for today:

1. _____

2. _____

3. _____

4. _____

5. _____

Do not be conformed to this world, but be transformed by the renewal of your mind, that by testing you may discern what is the will of God, what is good and acceptable and perfect. (ESV)

Don't become so well-adjusted to your culture that you fit into it without even thinking. Instead, fix your attention on God. You'll be changed from the inside out. Readily recognize what he wants from you, and quickly respond to it. Unlike the culture around you, always dragging you down to its level of immaturity, God brings the best out of you, develops well-formed maturity in you. (MSG)

Underline, highlight, doodle your initial thoughts and notes as you read the passage.

_____

_____

_____

_____

_____

_____

_____

What does Paul tell us NOT to be?

_____ to this world (ESV)

So _____ to your _____ that you
_____ without even _____ (MSG)

What does "conform" mean (it's okay to look it up)?

_____

_____

_____

What does it look like to be "conformed" or "so well-adjusted" to this
world/culture? Try to think of specific examples.

_____

_____

_____

_____

Why is it a bad thing? Why does it matter?

_____

_____

_____

_____

What does Paul tell us we should do instead?

_____

_____

_____

What does "transformed" mean (it's okay to look it up)?

_____

_____

_____

What would it practically look like?

_____

_____

_____

_____

_____

_____

What is the result of this better way of being?

_____

_____

_____

_____

Practically, what would this look like in our lives?

_____

_____

_____

_____

6 Take action.

What is one thing you can do today to go take action with regard to your new way of thinking (from steps 2 and 3)?

_____

_____

_____

_____

_____

_____

_____

7 Close in prayer, thanking God in advance for renewal and transformation.

Day 3: _____

1 Pray for wisdom & mind renewal.

You can use the prayer on page 15 as a starting point if you aren't sure where to begin.

2 Take every thought not of God Captive.

What toxic thoughts, worries, anxieties, fears, sin struggles, impossible barriers are standing in your way today? What is currently taking first place in your life over God? Jot your notes down below and put them in the left hand columns on the following page.

_____
_____
_____
_____
_____

3 Replace the lies with God's truth and Word.

In the right hand column on the following page, insert God's truth in place of lies or worldly patterns you captured. Space is also provided to journal below as you capture these thoughts/patterns and give them to God. Take time to Google "Bible verses about _____" (fear, anxiety, depression, pain, loss, insecurity, pride, unforgiveness, etc.) if you need to look up a truth about something you are struggling with. We also have some verses by category at www.butGodMinistry.com/GodsTruth

_____
_____
_____
_____
_____
_____

Thoughts/patterns not of God	God's TRUTH to claim/overcome

Reflect upon the following in your life right now:
(Jot down any that apply that you can think of in these categories
from Philippians 4:8)

What is...	
True Honorable Just Pure Lovely Commendable Excellent Praiseworthy	

4 Five things I am grateful for today:

1. _____

2. _____

3. _____

4. _____

5. _____

5 Today's Scripture – Romans 12:3

For by the grace given to me I say to everyone among you not to think of himself more highly than he ought to think, but to think with sober judgment, each according to the measure of faith that God has assigned. (ESV)

I'm speaking to you out of deep gratitude for all that God has given me, and especially as I have responsibilities in relation to you. Living then, as every one of you does, in pure grace, it's important that you not misinterpret yourselves as people who are bringing this goodness to God. No, God brings it all to you. The only accurate way to understand ourselves is by what God is and by what he does for us, not by what we are and what we do for him. (MSG)

Underline, highlight, doodle your initial thoughts and notes as you read the passage.

_____

_____

_____

_____

_____

_____

_____

What is the foundation from which Paul says he is speaking to the Romans?

> ...by the _____ given to me (ESV)

> I'm speaking to you out of deep _____ for
> all that God has _____ (MSG)

Why do you think this is foundational for what he wants to tell them (us)?

_____

_____

_____

_____

What is Paul's instruction as to what they (we) are NOT to do?

_____

_____

_____

_____

Instead what should they (we) do/think?

_____

_____

_____

_____

What does "sober judgment" mean? In what ways would you describe this type of judgment (think about some synonyms or examples)?

_____

_____

_____

How are we equipped to do this?

_____
_____
_____
_____

What does "measure of faith that God has assigned" mean?

_____
_____
_____
_____
_____
_____

Practically, what would this look like in your life? What would you do differently?

_____
_____
_____
_____
_____
_____
_____
_____

6 Take action.

What is one thing you can do today to go take action with regard to your new way of thinking (from steps 2 and 3)?

_____

_____

_____

_____

_____

_____

_____

_____

7 Close in prayer, thanking God in advance for renewal and transformation.

Day 4: _____

1 Pray for wisdom & mind renewal.
You can use the prayer on page 15 as a starting point if you aren't sure where to begin.

2 Take every thought not of God Captive.
What toxic thoughts, worries, anxieties, fears, sin struggles, impossible barriers are standing in your way today? What is currently taking first place in your life over God? Jot your notes down below and put them in the left hand columns on the following page.

_____

_____

_____

_____

_____

3 Replace the lies with God's truth and Word.
In the right hand column on the following page, insert God's truth in place of lies or worldly patterns you captured. Space is also provided to journal below as you capture these thoughts/patterns and give them to God. Take time to Google "Bible verses about _____" (fear, anxiety, depression, pain, loss, insecurity, pride, unforgiveness, etc.) if you need to look up a truth about something you are struggling with. We also have some verses by category at www.butGodMinistry.com/GodsTruth

_____

_____

_____

_____

_____

_____

Thoughts/patterns not of God   God's TRUTH to claim/overcome

Reflect upon the following in your life right now:
(Jot down any that apply that you can think of in these categories
from Philippians 4:8)

What is...	
True Honorable Just Pure Lovely Commendable Excellent Praiseworthy	

4 Five things I am grateful for today:

1. _____

2. _____

3. _____

4. _____

5. _____

5 Today's Scripture – Romans 12:4-5

For as in one body we have many members, and the members do not all have the same function, so we, though many, are one body in Christ, and individually members one of another. (ESV)

In this way we are like the various parts of a human body. Each part gets its meaning from the body as a whole, not the other way around. The body we're talking about is Christ's body of chosen people. Each of us finds our meaning and function as a part of his body. But as a chopped-off finger or cut-off toe we wouldn't amount to much, would we? So since we find ourselves fashioned into all these excellently formed and marvelously functioning parts in Christ's body, let's just go ahead and be what we were made to be, without enviously or pridefully comparing ourselves with each other, or trying to be something we aren't.(MSG)

Underline, highlight, doodle your initial thoughts and notes as you read the passage.

_____

_____

_____

_____

_____

What does Paul compare the church to?

One _____ with many _____ (ESV)

Various _____ of a human _____ (MSG)

The Message translation goes on to say where each part gets it meaning:

_____

_____

The Message then clarifies that the body we're talking about is:

Christ's _____ of _____ people.

The Messages says that each of us find our _____ and
_____ as part of the body.

What does it mean to find our meaning and function as part of the body?

_____

_____

_____

_____

The ESV translations says that the members of the body do not all have
the same _____. So at the same time we are
_____ body in Christ, and _____ members one
of another.

How does the Message conclude this passage? What does it say we should do and not do?

_____
_____
_____
_____

Practically, what would this look like in your life? How would you live differently?

_____
_____
_____
_____

6 Take action.

What is one thing you can do today to go take action with regard to your new way of thinking (from steps 2 and 3)?

_____
_____
_____
_____
_____
_____
_____

7 Close in prayer, thanking God in advance for renewal and transformation.

Day 5: _____

1 Pray for wisdom & mind renewal.

You can use the prayer on page 15 as a starting point if you aren't sure where to begin.

2 Take every thought not of God Captive.

What toxic thoughts, worries, anxieties, fears, sin struggles, impossible barriers are standing in your way today? What is currently taking first place in your life over God? Jot your notes down below and put them in the left hand columns on the following page.

_____

_____

_____

_____

_____

3 Replace the lies with God's truth and Word.

In the right hand column on the following page, insert God's truth in place of lies or worldly patterns you captured. Space is also provided to journal below as you capture these thoughts/patterns and give them to God. Take time to Google "Bible verses about _____" (fear, anxiety, depression, pain, loss, insecurity, pride, unforgiveness, etc.) if you need to look up a truth about something you are struggling with. We also have some verses by category at www.butGodMinistry.com/GodsTruth

_____

_____

_____

_____

_____

_____

Thoughts/patterns not of God	God's TRUTH to claim/overcome

Reflect upon the following in your life right now:
(Jot down any that apply that you can think of in these categories
from Philippians 4:8)

What is...	
True Honorable Just Pure Lovely Commendable Excellent Praiseworthy	

4 Five things I am grateful for today:

1. _____

2. _____

3. _____

4. _____

5. _____

Today's Scripture – Romans 12:6-8

Having gifts that differ according to the grace given to us, let us use them: if prophecy, in proportion to our faith; if service, in our serving; the one who teaches, in his teaching; the one who exhorts, in his exhortation; the one who contributes, in generosity; the one who leads, with zeal; the one who does acts of mercy, with cheerfulness. (ESV)

If you preach, just preach God's Message, nothing else; if you help, just help, don't take over; if you teach, stick to your teaching; if you give encouraging guidance, be careful that you don't get bossy; if you're put in charge, don't manipulate; if you're called to give aid to people in distress, keep your eyes open and be quick to respond; if you work with the disadvantaged, don't let yourself get irritated with them or depressed by them. Keep a smile on your face. (MSG)

Underline, highlight, doodle your initial thoughts and notes as you read the passage.

_____

_____

_____

_____

_____

_____

In this passage, Paul is pointing out that we all have different _____.

And these gifts differ according to the _____ given to us.

What does "grace" mean (it's okay to look it up)?

_____

_____

_____

_____

Why do you think he says "according to the grace given to us" when talking about our gifts? Why would it be significant?

_____

_____

_____

_____

Paul's command with regard to these gifts is, "let us _____ them."

List out the different gifts Paul cites in the passage, along with ways we should use them:

_____

_____

_____

_____

_____

_____

_____

_____

_____

_____

What point is Paul making about our gifts and how we should use them?

_____

_____

_____

_____

What are some of the gifts God has given you? Really spend some time thinking about this and talking to God about it.

_____

_____

_____

_____

Where along the scale do you feel like you are currently using gifts given to you by God?

⬅——————————————————————➡

Not using   Using them, but   Fully using them
them at all   for my glory   for God's kingdom

In what ways are you currently using the gifts you have been given?

_____

_____

_____

_____

In what ways could you start to use the gifts you have been given for God's glory and kingdom?

_____

_____

_____

_____

6 Take action.

What is one thing you can do today to go take action with regard to your new way of thinking (from steps 2 and 3)?

_____

_____

_____

_____

_____

_____

_____

_____

7 Close in prayer, thanking God in advance for renewal and transformation.

Day 6: _____

1 Pray for wisdom & mind renewal.

You can use the prayer on page 15 as a starting point if you aren't sure where to begin.

2 Take every thought not of God Captive.

What toxic thoughts, worries, anxieties, fears, sin struggles, impossible barriers are standing in your way today? What is currently taking first place in your life over God? Jot your notes down below and put them in the left hand columns on the following page.

_____

_____

_____

_____

_____

3 Replace the lies with God's truth and Word.

In the right hand column on the following page, insert God's truth in place of lies or worldly patterns you captured. Space is also provided to journal below as you capture these thoughts/patterns and give them to God. Take time to Google "Bible verses about _____" (fear, anxiety, depression, pain, loss, insecurity, pride, unforgiveness, etc.) if you need to look up a truth about something you are struggling with. We also have some verses by category at www.butGodMinistry.com/GodsTruth

_____

_____

_____

_____

_____

_____

Thoughts/patterns not of God	God's TRUTH to claim/overcome

Reflect upon the following in your life right now:
(Jot down any that apply that you can think of in these categories from Philippians 4:8)

What is...	
True Honorable Just Pure Lovely Commendable Excellent Praiseworthy	

4 Five things I am grateful for today:

1. _____

2. _____

3. _____

4. _____

5. _____

5 Today's Scripture – Romans 12:9

Let love be genuine. Abhor what is evil; hold fast to what is good. (ESV)

Love from the center of who you are; don't fake it. Run for dear life from evil; hold on for dear life to good. (MSG)

Underline, highlight, doodle your initial thoughts and notes as you read the passage.

_____
_____
_____
_____
_____
_____
_____

Paul teaches that our love should be what? _____(ESV)

The Message translation says to love from the center of what?

_____

...to not _____ it. (MSG)

What does genuine love look like? What does it look like to love from the "center of who you are?"

_____
_____
_____
_____

What does faking it look like?

_____
_____
_____
_____

How genuinely do you love others?

_____
_____
_____

Paul continues telling us to _____ what is evil (ESV).

What does "abhor" mean (it's okay if you have to look it up)?

_____
_____
_____

How does the Message translation describe it?

_____

_____

_____

But it isn't just abhorring and running for dear life from evil. What else should we do?

_____ to what is good. (ESV)

_____ to good (MSG)

Practically, what would it look like to run from evil?

_____

_____

_____

_____

Practically, what would it look like to hold fast / hold on for dear life to good?

_____

_____

_____

_____

Is more of your time spent holding onto evil or good?

_____

_____

_____

6 Take action.

What is one thing you can do today to go take action with regard to your new way of thinking (from steps 2 and 3)?

_____

_____

_____

_____

_____

_____

_____

_____

7 Close in prayer, thanking God in advance for renewal and transformation.

Day 7: _____

1 Pray for wisdom & mind renewal.

You can use the prayer on page 15 as a starting point if you aren't sure where to begin.

2 Take every thought not of God Captive.

What toxic thoughts, worries, anxieties, fears, sin struggles, impossible barriers are standing in your way today? What is currently taking first place in your life over God? Jot your notes down below and put them in the left hand columns on the following page.

_____

_____

_____

_____

_____

3 Replace the lies with God's truth and Word.

In the right hand column on the following page, insert God's truth in place of lies or worldly patterns you captured. Space is also provided to journal below as you capture these thoughts/patterns and give them to God. Take time to Google "Bible verses about _____" (fear, anxiety, depression, pain, loss, insecurity, pride, unforgiveness, etc.) if you need to look up a truth about something you are struggling with. We also have some verses by category at www.butGodMinistry.com/GodsTruth

_____

_____

_____

_____

_____

_____

Thoughts/patterns not of God   God's TRUTH to claim/overcome

Reflect upon the following in your life right now:
(Jot down any that apply that you can think of in these categories
from Philippians 4:8)

What is...	
True Honorable Just Pure Lovely Commendable Excellent Praiseworthy	

4 Five things I am grateful for today:

1. _____

2. _____

3. _____

4. _____

5. _____

5 Today's Scripture – Romans 12:10

Love one another with brotherly affection. Outdo one another in showing honor. (ESV)

Be good friends who love deeply; practice playing second fiddle. (MSG)

Underline, highlight, doodle your initial thoughts and notes as you read the passage.

_____
_____
_____
_____
_____
_____
_____

How does Paul say we should love one another?

With _____ (ESV)

The Message translation says to be _____ who

_____ deeply.

Practically, what would this look like in our lives to be the kind of friends who love deeply?

_____
_____
_____
_____

Paul says we should OUTDO one another in what?

_____ (ESV)

The Message translations says we should PRACTICE what?

...playing _____ (MSG)

Practically what does it look like to outdo one another in showing honor?

_____
_____
_____
_____

What are some practical examples you have seen of those that are really great at honoring others and playing "second fiddle"?

_____

_____

_____

_____

_____

_____

6 Take action.

What is one thing you can do today to go take action with regard to your new way of thinking (from steps 2 and 3)?

_____

_____

_____

_____

_____

_____

_____

7 Close in prayer, thanking God in advance for renewal and transformation.

Day 8: _____

1 Pray for wisdom & mind renewal.

You can use the prayer on page 15 as a starting point if you aren't sure where to begin.

2 Take every thought not of God Captive.

What toxic thoughts, worries, anxieties, fears, sin struggles, impossible barriers are standing in your way today? What is currently taking first place in your life over God? Jot your notes down below and put them in the left hand columns on the following page.

_____

_____

_____

_____

_____

3 Replace the lies with God's truth and Word.

In the right hand column on the following page, insert God's truth in place of lies or worldly patterns you captured. Space is also provided to journal below as you capture these thoughts/patterns and give them to God. Take time to Google "Bible verses about _____" (fear, anxiety, depression, pain, loss, insecurity, pride, unforgiveness, etc.) if you need to look up a truth about something you are struggling with. We also have some verses by category at www.butGodMinistry.com/GodsTruth

_____

_____

_____

_____

_____

_____

Thoughts/patterns not of God	God's TRUTH to claim/overcome

Reflect upon the following in your life right now:
(Jot down any that apply that you can think of in these categories
from Philippians 4:8)

What is...	
True Honorable Just Pure Lovely Commendable Excellent Praiseworthy	

4 Five things I am grateful for today:

1. _____

2. _____

3. _____

4. _____

5. _____

5 Today's Scripture – Romans 12:11

Do not be slothful in zeal, be fervent in spirit, serve the Lord. (ESV)

Don't burn out; keep yourselves fueled and aflame. Be alert servants of the Master, cheerfully expectant.(MSG)

Underline, highlight, doodle your initial thoughts and notes as you read the passage.

Recap the initial command in this passage:

Do not be _____ in _____ (ESV)

What does "slothful" mean (it is okay to look it up)?

_____
_____
_____

What does "zeal" mean (it is okay to look it up)?

_____
_____
_____

What would it look like to be slothful in zeal?

_____
_____
_____

The Message translation puts it:

...don't _____ (MSG)

Why do you think this was important for Paul to point out?

_____
_____
_____

* * *

The other end of the "do not" is what we should do instead. How do both translations state it?

Be _____ in spirit (ESV)

Keep yourselves _____ and _____ (MSG)

What does "fervent" mean (it is okay to look it up)?

_____
_____
_____

What would it look like for someone to be fervent in spirit?

_____
_____
_____
_____

What are practical ways you can keep yourself fueled and aflame to use your gifts for God's kingdom and love others well?

_____
_____
_____
_____

Paul continues saying we should do what?

_____ the Lord (ESV)

Be alert _____ of the Master (MSG)

The Message continues saying we should be _____
expectant.

What does "expectant" mean (it is okay to look it up)?

_____

_____

_____

Practically what would it look like in your life to be CHEERFULLY
EXPECTANT?

_____

_____

_____

_____

6 Take action.

What is one thing you can do today to go take action with regard to your
new way of thinking (from steps 2 and 3)?

_____

_____

_____

_____

_____

_____

_____

_____

7 Close in prayer, thanking God in advance for
renewal and transformation.

• • •

Day 9: _____

1 Pray for wisdom & mind renewal.
You can use the prayer on page 15 as a starting point if you aren't sure where to begin.

2 Take every thought not of God Captive.
What toxic thoughts, worries, anxieties, fears, sin struggles, impossible barriers are standing in your way today? What is currently taking first place in your life over God? Jot your notes down below and put them in the left hand columns on the following page.

_____

_____

_____

_____

_____

3 Replace the lies with God's truth and Word.
In the right hand column on the following page, insert God's truth in place of lies or worldly patterns you captured. Space is also provided to journal below as you capture these thoughts/patterns and give them to God. Take time to Google "Bible verses about _____" (fear, anxiety, depression, pain, loss, insecurity, pride, unforgiveness, etc.) if you need to look up a truth about something you are struggling with. We also have some verses by category at www.butGodMinistry.com/GodsTruth

_____

_____

_____

_____

_____

_____

Thoughts/patterns not of God   God's TRUTH to claim/overcome

Reflect upon the following in your life right now:

(Jot down any that apply that you can think of in these categories from Philippians 4:8)

What is...	
True Honorable Just Pure Lovely Commendable Excellent Praiseworthy	

4 Five things I am grateful for today:

1. _____

2. _____

3. _____

4. _____

5. _____

5 Today's Scripture – Romans 12:12

Rejoice in hope, be patient in tribulation, be constant in prayer. (ESV)

Don't quit in hard times; pray all the harder. (MSG)

Underline, highlight, doodle your initial thoughts and notes as you read the passage.

_____
_____
_____
_____
_____
_____
_____

In the ESV translation, Paul tells us to do the following:

_____ in _____,

...be _____ in _____,

...be _____ in prayer _____.

Let's dig into some of these words for a fuller appreciation of what Paul is saying. Look up (or describe in your own words) the following:

Rejoice:

_____

_____

Hope:

_____

_____

Patient:

_____

_____

Tribulation:

_____

_____

Constant:

_____

_____

What would it look like to REJOICE in HOPE?

_____

_____

_____

_____

What would it look like to be PATIENT in TRIBULATION?

_____

_____

_____

_____

What would it look like to be CONSTANT in PRAYER?

_____

_____

_____

_____

The Message translation states it as follows:

...don't _____ in _____ times;

_____ all the _____.

6 Take action.

What is one thing you can do today to go take action with regard to your new way of thinking (from steps 2 and 3)?

_____

_____

_____

_____

_____

_____

_____

_____

7 Close in prayer, thanking God in advance for renewal and transformation.

Day 10: _____

1 Pray for wisdom & mind renewal.
You can use the prayer on page 15 as a starting point if you aren't sure where to begin.

2 Take every thought not of God Captive.
What toxic thoughts, worries, anxieties, fears, sin struggles, impossible barriers are standing in your way today? What is currently taking first place in your life over God? Jot your notes down below and put them in the left hand columns on the following page.

_____

_____

_____

_____

_____

3 Replace the lies with God's truth and Word.
In the right hand column on the following page, insert God's truth in place of lies or worldly patterns you captured. Space is also provided to journal below as you capture these thoughts/patterns and give them to God. Take time to Google "Bible verses about _____" (fear, anxiety, depression, pain, loss, insecurity, pride, unforgiveness, etc.) if you need to look up a truth about something you are struggling with. We also have some verses by category at www.butGodMinistry.com/GodsTruth

_____

_____

_____

_____

_____

_____

Thoughts/patterns not of God	God's TRUTH to claim/overcome

Reflect upon the following in your life right now:
(Jot down any that apply that you can think of in these categories
from Philippians 4:8)

What is...	
True	
Honorable	
Just	
Pure	
Lovely	
Commendable	
Excellent	
Praiseworthy	

4 Five things I am grateful for today:

1. _____

2. _____

3. _____

4. _____

5. _____

5 Today's Scripture – Romans 12:13

Contribute to the needs of the saints and seek to show hospitality. (ESV)

Help needy Christians; be inventive in hospitality. (MSG)

Underline, highlight, doodle your initial thoughts and notes as you read the passage.

_____

_____

_____

_____

_____

_____

_____

Paul's next set of instructions are to:

_____ to the _____ of the saints (ESV)

Help _____ Christians (MSG)

He further says we should seek to show _____ (ESV)

The Message translation says to be _____
in hospitality.

How does the idea of being "inventive" in hospitality change the way you look at Paul's instructions?

_____
_____
_____
_____
_____
_____

Why do you think showing hospitality is important in Christian community?

_____
_____
_____
_____

Practically, what would it look like in your life to help those in need and to show hospitality?

_____

_____

_____

_____

_____

_____

6 Take action.

What is one thing you can do today to go take action with regard to your new way of thinking (from steps 2 and 3)?

_____

_____

_____

_____

_____

_____

_____

7 Close in prayer, thanking God in advance for renewal and transformation.

Day 11: _____

1 Pray for wisdom & mind renewal.
You can use the prayer on page 15 as a starting point if you aren't sure
where to begin.

2 Take every thought not of God Captive.
What toxic thoughts, worries, anxieties, fears, sin struggles, impossible
barriers are standing in your way today? What is currently taking first
place in your life over God? Jot your notes down below and put them in
the left hand columns on the following page.

_____

_____

_____

_____

_____

3 Replace the lies with God's truth and Word.
In the right hand column on the following page, insert God's truth in place
of lies or worldly patterns you captured. Space is also provided to journal
below as you capture these thoughts/patterns and give them to God.
Take time to Google "Bible verses about _____" (fear, anxiety,
depression, pain, loss, insecurity, pride, unforgiveness, etc.) if you need to
look up a truth about something you are struggling with. We also have
some verses by category at www.butGodMinistry.com/GodsTruth

_____

_____

_____

_____

_____

_____

● ● ●

Thoughts/patterns not of God   God's TRUTH to claim/overcome

Reflect upon the following in your life right now:

(Jot down any that apply that you can think of in these categories from Philippians 4:8)

What is...	
True Honorable Just Pure Lovely Commendable Excellent Praiseworthy	

4 Five things I am grateful for today:

1. _____

2. _____

3. _____

4. _____

5. _____

5 Today's Scripture – Romans 12:14

Bless those who persecute you; bless and do not curse them. (ESV)

Bless your enemies; no cursing under your breath. (MSG)

Underline, highlight, doodle your initial thoughts and notes as you read the passage.

Paul offers some tough instructions here. He says to:

_____ those who _____ you. (ESV)

The Message translates it as _____ your _____.

He further says to bless and not _____ them (ESV),

or as the Message translates, no _____
under your breath.

What does "bless" mean (it is okay to look it up)?

_____

_____

_____

The Bible tells us trials and persecution will come. Just because we are living out our Christian faith does not mean we can avoid hardships. In fact, the Bible tells us to expect it. We don't have to approve of or condone harsh and unfair treatment. We don't have to remain in toxic environments. However, the Bible tells us we should bless those who persecute us.

Practically, what would this look like in our lives to bless those who persecute us?

_____

_____

_____

_____

_____

Why would this be an important part of living out our Christian faith?

_____

_____

_____

_____

6 Take action.

What is one thing you can do today to go take action with regard to your new way of thinking (from steps 2 and 3)?

_____

_____

_____

_____

_____

_____

_____

_____

7 Close in prayer, thanking God in advance for renewal and transformation.

Day 12: _____

1 Pray for wisdom & mind renewal.
You can use the prayer on page 15 as a starting point if you aren't sure where to begin.

2 Take every thought not of God Captive.
What toxic thoughts, worries, anxieties, fears, sin struggles, impossible barriers are standing in your way today? What is currently taking first place in your life over God? Jot your notes down below and put them in the left hand columns on the following page.

_____

_____

_____

_____

_____

3 Replace the lies with God's truth and Word.
In the right hand column on the following page, insert God's truth in place of lies or worldly patterns you captured. Space is also provided to journal below as you capture these thoughts/patterns and give them to God. Take time to Google "Bible verses about _____" (fear, anxiety, depression, pain, loss, insecurity, pride, unforgiveness, etc.) if you need to look up a truth about something you are struggling with. We also have some verses by category at www.butGodMinistry.com/GodsTruth

_____

_____

_____

_____

_____

_____

Thoughts/patterns not of God	God's TRUTH to claim/overcome

Reflect upon the following in your life right now:
(Jot down any that apply that you can think of in these categories from Philippians 4:8)

What is...	
True Honorable Just Pure Lovely Commendable Excellent Praiseworthy	

4 Five things I am grateful for today:

1. _____

2. _____

3. _____

4. _____

5. _____

5 Today's Scripture – Romans 12:15

Rejoice with those who rejoice, weep with those who weep. (ESV)

Laugh with your happy friends when they're happy; share tears when they're down. (MSG)

Underline, highlight, doodle your initial thoughts and notes as you read the passage.

_____

_____

_____

_____

_____

_____

_____

In this passage, Paul tells us to:

_____ with those who _____,

_____ with those who _____ (ESV)

The Message translation says:

_____ with your happy friends when they're happy;

share _____ when they're down. (MSG)

Why is it important that we share both rejoicing and tears with our friends?

_____

_____

_____

_____

_____

It seems like a fairly easy set of instructions, but in reality, it isn't always that easy to do. What kinds of things or mindsets or perceptions or lies we believe can make it hard for us to join our friends in their rejoicing or tears?

_____

_____

_____

_____

_____

Which is harder for you: to rejoice with happy friends or cry with sad friends? Why?

_____

_____

_____

_____

Practically, what would this look like in your life to be the kind of friend who could be counted on in times of both rejoicing and sorrow?

_____

_____

_____

_____

6 Take action.

What is one thing you can do today to go take action with regard to your new way of thinking (from steps 2 and 3)?

_____

_____

_____

_____

_____

_____

_____

7 Close in prayer, thanking God in advance for renewal and transformation.

Day 13: _____

1 Pray for wisdom & mind renewal.
You can use the prayer on page 15 as a starting point if you aren't sure where to begin.

2 Take every thought not of God Captive.
What toxic thoughts, worries, anxieties, fears, sin struggles, impossible barriers are standing in your way today? What is currently taking first place in your life over God? Jot your notes down below and put them in the left hand columns on the following page.

_____

_____

_____

_____

_____

3 Replace the lies with God's truth and Word.
In the right hand column on the following page, insert God's truth in place of lies or worldly patterns you captured. Space is also provided to journal below as you capture these thoughts/patterns and give them to God. Take time to Google "Bible verses about _____" (fear, anxiety, depression, pain, loss, insecurity, pride, unforgiveness, etc.) if you need to look up a truth about something you are struggling with. We also have some verses by category at www.butGodMinistry.com/GodsTruth

_____

_____

_____

_____

_____

Thoughts/patterns not of God	God's TRUTH to claim/overcome

Reflect upon the following in your life right now:

(Jot down any that apply that you can think of in these categories
from Philippians 4:8)

What is...	
True
Honorable
Just
Pure
Lovely
Commendable
Excellent
Praiseworthy	

4 Five things I am grateful for today:

4. _____

5. _____

6. _____

7. _____

8. _____

5 Today's Scripture – Romans 12:16

Live in harmony with one another. Do not be haughty, but associate with the lowly. Never be wise in your own sight. (ESV)

Get along with each other; don't be stuck-up. Make friends with nobodies; don't be the great somebody. (MSG)

Underline, highlight, doodle your initial thoughts and notes as you read the passage.

_____
_____
_____
_____
_____
_____
_____

Paul tells us to live in _____ with one another (ESV).

The Message translates it as _____
with each other (MSG).

What does "harmony" mean (it is okay to look it up)?

_____

_____

_____

What would it look like to live in HARMONY with one another?

_____

_____

_____

Paul further instructs us to not be _____ (ESV)

What does "haughty" mean (it is okay to look it up)?

_____

_____

_____

The Message translation says, don't be _____.

What does it look like to be haughty/stuck-up?

_____

_____

_____

Instead, Paul says to associate with the _____ (ESV).

What does "lowly" mean (it is okay to look it up)?

_____

_____

_____

The Message translation says to make friends with _____.

He goes on to say, never be wise in _____ (ESV),

or as the Message phrases it, don't be the

_____. (MSG)

How do you see living in harmony, not being haughty/stuck-up, and associating with the lowly are linked together?

_____

_____

_____

_____

Practically, what would living this out look like in your life?

_____

_____

_____

_____

_____

_____

6 Take action.

What is one thing you can do today to go take action with regard to your new way of thinking (from steps 2 and 3)?

_____

_____

_____

_____

_____

_____

_____

_____

7 Close in prayer, thanking God in advance for renewal and transformation.

Day 14: _____

1 Pray for wisdom & mind renewal.

You can use the prayer on page 15 as a starting point if you aren't sure where to begin.

2 Take every thought not of God Captive.

What toxic thoughts, worries, anxieties, fears, sin struggles, impossible barriers are standing in your way today? What is currently taking first place in your life over God? Jot your notes down below and put them in the left hand columns on the following page.

_____

_____

_____

_____

_____

3 Replace the lies with God's truth and Word.

In the right hand column on the following page, insert God's truth in place of lies or worldly patterns you captured. Space is also provided to journal below as you capture these thoughts/patterns and give them to God. Take time to Google "Bible verses about _____" (fear, anxiety, depression, pain, loss, insecurity, pride, unforgiveness, etc.) if you need to look up a truth about something you are struggling with. We also have some verses by category at www.butGodMinistry.com/GodsTruth

_____

_____

_____

_____

_____

_____

Thoughts/patterns not of God	God's TRUTH to claim/overcome

Reflect upon the following in your life right now:
(Jot down any that apply that you can think of in these categories
from Philippians 4:8)

What is...	
True Honorable Just Pure Lovely Commendable Excellent Praiseworthy	

4 Five things I am grateful for today:

1. _____

2. _____

3. _____

4. _____

5. _____

5 Today's Scripture – Romans 12:17

Repay no one evil for evil, but give thought to do what is honorable in the sight of all. (ESV)

Don't hit back; discover beauty in everyone. (MSG)

Underline, highlight, doodle your initial thoughts and notes as you read the passage.

_____

_____

_____

_____

_____

_____

_____

Paul tells us we should repay no one evil for _____ (ESV)

The Message states it as "don't _____" (MSG)

What does Paul mean by repaying evil for evil or hitting back?

_____

_____

_____

_____

Instead, Paul tells us to:

...give thought to what is _____ in the sight of all. (ESV)

...to discover _____ in _____ (MSG)

What does "honorable" mean (it is okay to look it up)?

_____

_____

_____

Why do you think the two concepts (not repaying evil for evil + doing what is honorable in the sight of all / discovering beauty in everyone) are linked here by Paul?

_____

_____

_____

_____

_____

Practically, what would living out these instructions look like in your life?

_____

_____

_____

_____

_____

_____

6 Take action.

What is one thing you can do today to go take action with regard to your new way of thinking (from steps 2 and 3)?

_____

_____

_____

_____

_____

_____

_____

7 Close in prayer, thanking God in advance for renewal and transformation.

Day 15: _____

1 Pray for wisdom & mind renewal.

You can use the prayer on page 15 as a starting point if you aren't sure where to begin.

2 Take every thought not of God Captive.

What toxic thoughts, worries, anxieties, fears, sin struggles, impossible barriers are standing in your way today? What is currently taking first place in your life over God? Jot your notes down below and put them in the left hand columns on the following page.

_____

_____

_____

_____

_____

3 Replace the lies with God's truth and Word.

In the right hand column on the following page, insert God's truth in place of lies or worldly patterns you captured. Space is also provided to journal below as you capture these thoughts/patterns and give them to God. Take time to Google "Bible verses about _____" (fear, anxiety, depression, pain, loss, insecurity, pride, unforgiveness, etc.) if you need to look up a truth about something you are struggling with. We also have some verses by category at www.butGodMinistry.com/GodsTruth

_____

_____

_____

_____

_____

_____

Thoughts/patterns not of God	God's TRUTH to claim/overcome

Reflect upon the following in your life right now:
(Jot down any that apply that you can think of in these categories from Philippians 4:8)

What is... True Honorable Just Pure Lovely Commendable Excellent Praiseworthy	

4 Five things I am grateful for today:

1. _____

2. _____

3. _____

4. _____

5. _____

5 Today's Scripture – Romans 12:18

If possible, so far as it depends on you, live peaceably with all. (ESV)

If you've got it in you, get along with everybody. (MSG)

Underline, highlight, doodle your initial thoughts and notes as you read the passage.

_____

_____

_____

_____

_____

_____

_____

What is Paul's action item in this passage?

Live _____ with _____ (ESV)

Get along with _____ (MSG)

What does "peaceably" mean (it is okay to look it up)?

_____

_____

_____

What two caveats does Paul give in the opening of this passage?

If _____, so far as it depends on _____ (ESV)

If you've _____ (MSG)

Why this caveat?

_____

_____

_____

Practically, what would living peaceably with all and getting along with everybody look like in your life?

_____

_____

_____

_____

6 Take action.

What is one thing you can do today to go take action with regard to your new way of thinking (from steps 2 and 3)?

_____

_____

_____

_____

_____

_____

_____

_____

7 Close in prayer, thanking God in advance for renewal and transformation.

Day 16: _____

1 Pray for wisdom & mind renewal.

You can use the prayer on page 15 as a starting point if you aren't sure where to begin.

2 Take every thought not of God Captive.

What toxic thoughts, worries, anxieties, fears, sin struggles, impossible barriers are standing in your way today? What is currently taking first place in your life over God? Jot your notes down below and put them in the left hand columns on the following page.

_____

_____

_____

_____

_____

3 Replace the lies with God's truth and Word.

In the right hand column on the following page, insert God's truth in place of lies or worldly patterns you captured. Space is also provided to journal below as you capture these thoughts/patterns and give them to God. Take time to Google "Bible verses about _____" (fear, anxiety, depression, pain, loss, insecurity, pride, unforgiveness, etc.) if you need to look up a truth about something you are struggling with. We also have some verses by category at www.butGodMinistry.com/GodsTruth

_____

_____

_____

_____

_____

_____

Thoughts/patterns not of God	God's TRUTH to claim/overcome

Reflect upon the following in your life right now:
(Jot down any that apply that you can think of in these categories
from Philippians 4:8)

What is...	
True Honorable Just Pure Lovely Commendable Excellent Praiseworthy	

4 Five things I am grateful for today:

1. _____

2. _____

3. _____

4. _____

5. _____

5 Today's Scripture – Romans 12:19

Beloved, never avenge yourselves, but leave it to the wrath of God, for it is written, "Vengeance is mine, I will repay, says the Lord." (ESV)

Don't insist on getting even; that's not for you to do. "I'll do the judging," says God. "I'll take care of it." (MSG)

Underline, highlight, doodle your initial thoughts and notes as you read the passage.

_____

_____

_____

_____

_____

_____

_____

What does Paul tell us not to do in this passage?

Never _____ yourselves (ESV)

Don't insist on getting _____; that's not for _____ to do (MSG)

What does "avenge" mean (it is okay to look it up)?

_____

_____

_____

What does Paul tell us to do instead?

Leave it to the _____ of _____ (ESV)

Paul quotes Scripture saying:

"Vengeance is _____, I will _____, says the Lord" (ESV)

"I'll do the _____," says God. "I'll take _____ of it." (MSG)

According to this Scripture, what does God promise He will do?

_____

_____

_____

How hard is it for you to let God do the judging and avenging for you?

_____

_____

_____

6 Take action.

What is one thing you can do today to go take action with regard to your new way of thinking (from steps 2 and 3)?

_____

_____

_____

_____

_____

_____

_____

7 Close in prayer, thanking God in advance for renewal and transformation.

Day 17: _____

1 Pray for wisdom & mind renewal.

You can use the prayer on page 15 as a starting point if you aren't sure where to begin.

2 Take every thought not of God Captive.

What toxic thoughts, worries, anxieties, fears, sin struggles, impossible barriers are standing in your way today? What is currently taking first place in your life over God? Jot your notes down below and put them in the left hand columns on the following page.

_____

_____

_____

_____

_____

3 Replace the lies with God's truth and Word.

In the right hand column on the following page, insert God's truth in place of lies or worldly patterns you captured. Space is also provided to journal below as you capture these thoughts/patterns and give them to God. Take time to Google "Bible verses about _____" (fear, anxiety, depression, pain, loss, insecurity, pride, unforgiveness, etc.) if you need to look up a truth about something you are struggling with. We also have some verses by category at www.butGodMinistry.com/GodsTruth

_____

_____

_____

_____

_____

_____

Thoughts/patterns not of God	God's TRUTH to claim/overcome

Reflect upon the following in your life right now:

(Jot down any that apply that you can think of in these categories from Philippians 4:8)

What is... True Honorable Just Pure Lovely Commendable Excellent Praiseworthy	

4 Five things I am grateful for today:

1. _____

2. _____

3. _____

4. _____

5. _____

5 Today's Scripture – Romans 12:20

To the contrary, "if your enemy is hungry, feed him; if he is thirsty, give him something to drink; for by so doing you will heap burning coals on his head." (ESV)

Our Scriptures tell us that if you see your enemy hungry, go buy that person lunch, or if he's thirsty, get him a drink. Your generosity will surprise him with goodness. (MSG)

Underline, highlight, doodle your initial thoughts and notes as you read the passage.

_____

_____

_____

_____

_____

_____

Still on the idea of not avenging ourselves and instead letting God take care of it, Paul instructs us on what to do instead.

If your enemy is hungry, _____; if he is thirsty

_____. (ESV)

So, not only does Paul tell us not to repay evil for evil and get even on our own, he tells us to look out for the needs of our enemies. He goes on to tell us why...

...by do doing you will _____

_____ (ESV).

That sounds harsh. What do you think he is trying to say?

_____

_____

_____

_____

The Message translation says it this way, "Your _____

will _____ him with _____ (MSG)

How do you see this playing out?

_____

_____

_____

_____

Is there anyone in your life you should be helping now instead of trying to get even with?

_____

_____

_____

_____

6 Take action.

What is one thing you can do today to go take action with regard to your new way of thinking (from steps 2 and 3)?

_____

_____

_____

_____

_____

_____

_____

7 Close in prayer, thanking God in advance for renewal and transformation.

Day 18: _____

1 Pray for wisdom & mind renewal.

You can use the prayer on page 15 as a starting point if you aren't sure where to begin.

2 Take every thought not of God Captive.

What toxic thoughts, worries, anxieties, fears, sin struggles, impossible barriers are standing in your way today? What is currently taking first place in your life over God? Jot your notes down below and put them in the left hand columns on the following page.

_____

_____

_____

_____

_____

3 Replace the lies with God's truth and Word.

In the right hand column on the following page, insert God's truth in place of lies or worldly patterns you captured. Space is also provided to journal below as you capture these thoughts/patterns and give them to God. Take time to Google "Bible verses about _____" (fear, anxiety, depression, pain, loss, insecurity, pride, unforgiveness, etc.) if you need to look up a truth about something you are struggling with. We also have some verses by category at www.butGodMinistry.com/GodsTruth

_____

_____

_____

_____

_____

_____

Thoughts/patterns not of God	God's TRUTH to claim/overcome

Reflect upon the following in your life right now:

(Jot down any that apply that you can think of in these categories from Philippians 4:8)

What is...	
True Honorable Just Pure Lovely Commendable Excellent Praiseworthy	

4 Five things I am grateful for today:

1. _____

2. _____

3. _____

4. _____

5. _____

5 Today's Scripture – Romans 12:21

Do not be overcome by evil, but overcome evil with good. (ESV)

Don't let evil get the best of you; get the best of evil by doing good. (MSG)

Underline, highlight, doodle your initial thoughts and notes as you read the passage.

_____

_____

_____

_____

_____

_____

_____

Remaining on the same theme of how we respond to adversity / evil / our enemies, Paul tells us the following:

Do not be _____ by _____ (ESV)

Don't let _____ get the _____ (MSG)

What does "being overcome" mean (it is okay to look it up)?

_____

_____

_____

What would it look like to be overcome by evil?

_____

_____

_____

Instead, Paul says we should:

Overcome _____ with _____ (ESV)

Get the best of _____ by doing _____ (MSG)

Why do you think this is a better way to live and respond?

_____

_____

_____

_____

How would your life look different by always overcoming evil with good?

_____

_____

_____

_____

6 Take action.
What is one thing you can do today to go take action with regard to your new way of thinking (from steps 2 and 3)?

_____

_____

_____

_____

_____

_____

_____

7 Close in prayer, thanking God in advance for renewal and transformation.

Day 19: _____

1 Pray for wisdom & mind renewal.

You can use the prayer on page 15 as a starting point if you aren't sure where to begin.

2 Take every thought not of God Captive.

What toxic thoughts, worries, anxieties, fears, sin struggles, impossible barriers are standing in your way today? What is currently taking first place in your life over God? Jot your notes down below and put them in the left hand columns on the following page.

_____

_____

_____

_____

_____

3 Replace the lies with God's truth and Word.

In the right hand column on the following page, insert God's truth in place of lies or worldly patterns you captured. Space is also provided to journal below as you capture these thoughts/patterns and give them to God. Take time to Google "Bible verses about _____" (fear, anxiety, depression, pain, loss, insecurity, pride, unforgiveness, etc.) if you need to look up a truth about something you are struggling with. We also have some verses by category at www.butGodMinistry.com/GodsTruth

_____

_____

_____

_____

_____

_____

Thoughts/patterns not of God	God's TRUTH to claim/overcome

Reflect upon the following in your life right now:

(Jot down any that apply that you can think of in these categories from Philippians 4:8)

What is... True Honorable Just Pure Lovely Commendable Excellent Praiseworthy	

4 Five things I am grateful for today:

1. _____

2. _____

3. _____

4. _____

5. _____

12:1 I appeal to you therefore, brothers, by the mercies of God, to present your bodies as a living sacrifice, holy and acceptable to God, which is your spiritual worship. (ESV)

So here's what I want you to do, God helping you: Take your everyday, ordinary life—your sleeping, eating, going-to-work, and walking-around life—and place it before God as an offering. Embracing what God does for you is the best thing you can do for him. (MSG)

12:2 Do not be conformed to this world, but be transformed by the renewal of your mind, that by testing you may discern what is the will of God, what is good and acceptable and perfect.

Don't become so well-adjusted to your culture that you fit into it without even thinking. Instead, fix your attention on God. You'll be changed from the inside out. Readily recognize what he wants from you, and quickly respond to it. Unlike the culture around you, always dragging you down to its level of immaturity, God brings the best out of you, develops well-formed maturity in you.

12:3 For by the grace given to me I say to everyone among you not to think of himself more highly than he ought to think, but to think with sober judgment, each according to the measure of faith that God has assigned.

I'm speaking to you out of deep gratitude for all that God has given me, and especially as I have responsibilities in relation to you. Living then, as every one of you does, in pure grace, it's important that you not misinterpret yourselves as people who are bringing this goodness to God. No, God brings it all to you. The only accurate way to understand ourselves is by what God is and by what he does for us, not by what we are and what we do for him.

* * *

We will spend the last three days of the 21-day renewal revisiting Romans 12. As you read through the first three verses again, underline, highlight, doodle your new thoughts and notes.

6 Take action.

What is one thing you can do today to go take action with regard to your new way of thinking (from steps 2 and 3)?

_____

_____

_____

_____

_____

_____

_____

7 Close in prayer, thanking God in advance for renewal and transformation.

Day 20: _____

1 Pray for wisdom & mind renewal.

You can use the prayer on page 15 as a starting point if you aren't sure where to begin.

2 Take every thought not of God Captive.

What toxic thoughts, worries, anxieties, fears, sin struggles, impossible barriers are standing in your way today? What is currently taking first place in your life over God? Jot your notes down below and put them in the left hand columns on the following page.

_____

_____

_____

_____

_____

3 Replace the lies with God's truth and Word.

In the right hand column on the following page, insert God's truth in place of lies or worldly patterns you captured. Space is also provided to journal below as you capture these thoughts/patterns and give them to God. Take time to Google "Bible verses about _____" (fear, anxiety, depression, pain, loss, insecurity, pride, unforgiveness, etc.) if you need to look up a truth about something you are struggling with. We also have some verses by category at www.butGodMinistry.com/GodsTruth

_____

_____

_____

_____

_____

_____

Thoughts/patterns not of God	God's TRUTH to claim/overcome

Reflect upon the following in your life right now:

(Jot down any that apply that you can think of in these categories from Philippians 4:8)

What is...	
True Honorable Just Pure Lovely Commendable Excellent Praiseworthy	

4 Five things I am grateful for today:

1. _____

2. _____

3. _____

4. _____

5. _____

Today's Scripture – Revisit Romans 12:4-11

12:4-5 For as in one body we have many members, and the members do not all have the same function, so we, though many, are one body in Christ, and individually members one of another. (ESV)

In this way we are like the various parts of a human body. Each part gets its meaning from the body as a whole, not the other way around. The body we're talking about is Christ's body of chosen people. Each of us finds our meaning and function as a part of his body. But as a chopped-off finger or cut-off toe we wouldn't amount to much, would we? So since we find ourselves fashioned into all these excellently formed and marvelously functioning parts in Christ's body, let's just go ahead and be what we were made to be, without enviously or pridefully comparing ourselves with each other, or trying to be something we aren't. (MSG)

12:6-8 Having gifts that differ according to the grace given to us, let us use them: if prophecy, in proportion to our faith; if service, in our serving; the one who teaches, in his teaching; the one who exhorts, in his exhortation; the one who contributes, in generosity; the one who leads, with zeal; the one who does acts of mercy, with cheerfulness.

If you preach, just preach God's Message, nothing else; if you help, just help, don't take over; if you teach, stick to your teaching; if you give encouraging guidance, be careful that you don't get bossy; if you're put in charge, don't manipulate; if you're called to give aid to people in distress, keep your eyes open and be quick to respond; if you work with the disadvantaged, don't let yourself get irritated with them or depressed by them. Keep a smile on your face.

12:9	Let love be genuine. Abhor what is evil; hold fast to what is good.	Love from the center of who you are; don't fake it. Run for dear life from evil; hold on for dear life to good.
12:10	Love one another with brotherly affection. Outdo one another in showing honor.	Be good friends who love deeply; practice playing second fiddle.
12:11	Do not be slothful in zeal, be fervent in spirit, serve the Lord.	Don't burn out; keep yourselves fueled and aflame. Be alert servants of the Master, cheerfully expectant.

We are spending the last three days of the 21-day renewal revisiting Romans 12. As you read through verses 4-11 again, underline, highlight, doodle your new thoughts and notes.

_____

_____

_____

_____

_____

_____

Have you had the opportunity to practice any of these new instructions from Paul recently?

_____

_____

_____

_____

_____

_____

_____

6 Take action.

What is one thing you can do today to go take action with regard to your new way of thinking (from steps 2 and 3)?

_____

_____

_____

_____

_____

_____

_____

_____

7 Close in prayer, thanking God in advance for renewal and transformation.

Day 21: _____

1 Pray for wisdom & mind renewal.

You can use the prayer on page 15 as a starting point if you aren't sure where to begin.

2 Take every thought not of God Captive.

What toxic thoughts, worries, anxieties, fears, sin struggles, impossible barriers are standing in your way today? What is currently taking first place in your life over God? Jot your notes down below and put them in the left hand columns on the following page.

_____

_____

_____

_____

_____

3 Replace the lies with God's truth and Word.

In the right hand column on the following page, insert God's truth in place of lies or worldly patterns you captured. Space is also provided to journal below as you capture these thoughts/patterns and give them to God. Take time to Google "Bible verses about _____" (fear, anxiety, depression, pain, loss, insecurity, pride, unforgiveness, etc.) if you need to look up a truth about something you are struggling with. We also have some verses by category at www.butGodMinistry.com/GodsTruth

_____

_____

_____

_____

_____

_____

Thoughts/patterns not of God	God's TRUTH to claim/overcome

Reflect upon the following in your life right now:

(Jot down any that apply that you can think of in these categories from Philippians 4:8)

What is...	
True Honorable Just Pure Lovely Commendable Excellent Praiseworthy	

4 Five things I am grateful for today:

1. _____

2. _____

3. _____

4. _____

5. _____

Today's Scripture – Revisit Romans 12:12-21

12:12 Rejoice in hope, be patient in tribulation, be constant in prayer. (ESV)

Don't quit in hard times; pray all the harder. (MSG)

12:13 Contribute to the needs of the saints and seek to show hospitality.

Help needy Christians; be inventive in hospitality.

12:14 Bless those who persecute you; bless and do not curse them.

Bless your enemies; no cursing under your breath.

12:15 Rejoice with those who rejoice, weep with those who weep.

Laugh with your happy friends when they're happy; share tears when they're down.

12:16 Live in harmony with one another. Do not be haughty, but associate with the lowly. Never be wise in your own sight.

Get along with each other; don't be stuck-up. Make friends with nobodies; don't be the great somebody.

12:17 Repay no one evil for evil, but give thought to do what is honorable in the sight of all.

Don't hit back; discover beauty in everyone.

12:18 If possible, so far as it depends on you, live peaceably with all.

If you've got it in you, get along with everybody.

12:19 Beloved, never avenge yourselves, but leave it to the wrath of God, for it is written, "Vengeance is mine, I will repay, says the Lord."

Don't insist on getting even; that's not for you to do. "I'll do the judging," says God. "I'll take care of it."

| 12:20 | To the contrary, "if your enemy is hungry, feed him; if he is thirsty, give him something to drink; for by so doing you will heap burning coals on his head." | Our Scriptures tell us that if you see your enemy hungry, go buy that person lunch, or if he's thirsty, get him a drink. Your generosity will surprise him with goodness. |
| 12:21 | Do not be overcome by evil, but overcome evil with good. | Don't let evil get the best of you; get the best of evil by doing good. |

We close out this 21-day renewal process reading verses 12-21 again. Underline, highlight, doodle your new thoughts and notes.

_____

_____

_____

_____

_____

_____

Have you had the opportunity to practice any of these new instructions from Paul recently?

_____

_____

_____

_____

_____

_____

_____

6 Take action.

What is one thing you can do today to go take action with regard to your new way of thinking (from steps 2 and 3)?

_____

_____

_____

_____

_____

_____

_____

_____

7 Close in prayer, thanking God in advance for renewal and transformation.

YOU DID IT!

We pray these 21 days and your intentional time with God renewing your mind has been transformational. We pray it is only the beginning of a lifetime dedicated to abiding in Jesus and becoming more and more like Him. We pray that you will continue to capture any thoughts not of God and replace them with God's truth.

We would love to hear your experience during the past 21 days. How has God worked on your mind? How has it changed your actions? How have you grown in relationship with Him? Please send us a message to info@butGodMinistry.com.

We have several other versions of 21-day renewals in the works. Visit www.butGodMinistry.com/RenewYourMind for updates and additional studies.

* * *

Made in the USA
Columbia, SC
02 April 2023